# A
# GUIDE
# TO
# SUCCESSFUL
# PUBLIC SPEAKING
## THE EASYWAY

HOWARD WADE
EASYWAY GUIDES

3

Easyway Guides
38 Cromwell Road
Walthamstow
London E17 9JN

© Straightforward Publishing 1998
first Edition

British Library cataloguing in Publication Data. A catalogue record is available for this book from the British Library.

ISBN 1900694 9 05

Printed by BPC Information Limited Exeter.

Cover design by Straightforward Graphics

# CONTENTS

# INTRODUCTION

Many times we have watched people stand up in front of others and deliver a speech or presentation. Politicians, actors, managers, a whole variety of people whose living depends on presenting to others in public. Often, the person speaking makes it look so effortless, as though speaking in front of others is the most natural thing in the world. For some it is. However, this book is designed for the majority who find public speaking and presenting in front of others a nerve wracking experience.

There are a number of key aspects which are fundamental to the art of public speaking and making presentations. Without a doubt the two most important are the person presenting and the nature of the material. This book concentrates heavily on these areas, offering invaluable advice.

In addition, advice on the use of visual aids and on the nature of the setting in which the public speaker will deliver his or her address is offered and also instruction on making the presentation and audience management.

Overall, this book will benefit those people who are new to the area of public speaking and making presentations. However, it will also benefit those who are more experienced but need a refresher on the art of presenting.

There are key points at the end of each chapter which help to reinforce the main areas.

Effective public speaking is an art and a skill and the rewards to those who can become effective presenters are enormous. It is hoped that this book will go some way to developing the skills and abilities needed.

# 1

# THE KEY ELEMENTS OF PUBLIC SPEAKING

Public speaking is very much an art and a skill which can be mastered by anyone. It is true to say that some people may be initially better equipped for the role of public speaker than others, by virtue of their own particular personality type. However, the truly effective public speaker learns the craft and applies certain techniques which generally derive from experience.

In this book I will be alluding to the person who has to deliver a speech or present a seminar, rather than the professional teacher. It is the person who is not constantly engaged in addressing groups who will most benefit from what is contained within.

## The person and the material

*There are two vital ingredients in public speaking. The first is very much the person delivering the speech or other material to a group. The second is the nature of the material being delivered.*

## The Person

For some people, standing in front of an audience, whatever the size, is not a real problem. For others however, the very thought of exposing oneself to a group of people, and being so vulnerable, is a nightmare best avoided.

When trying to put this into context it is important to remember that, when we communicate as part of a group, or simply on a one to one basis with another, then we interact primarily through speech and body language. We are often confident within ourselves because we feel secure in that we are part of a group interacting and that all eyes are not on us alone, at least not for a protracted period.

The situation is very different indeed when we are alone and faced with a group of people, strangers or not, and we have to present material. It means that we have to assume responsibility and take the lead and communicate successfully to others. Nervousness is very often the result when placed in this situation because, until we can make contact with the audience and establish a rapport, we are very much alone and feel vulnerable.

Obviously, there are a number of factors influencing the levels of confidence and differences in attitude between people, such as the nature and type of the person and their background, their past experience, both within the family and in the world of work and numerous other experiences besides. All these will affect a persons ability to become an effective public speaker.

This publication cannot completely erase your nervousness. It cannot change your personality overnight. However, what it can certainly do is to raise your awareness to the root of that feeling in the context of public speaking and to help you become more confident. It can also show you that, whatever your personality type, you can become a successful public speaker by applying certain fundamental techniques.

## Why do we feel nervous?

There are a number of reasons why we may feel nervous. You need to question yourself and ask yourself why. Was the sight of so many faces in front of you enough to frighten you and make you lose your self confidence or are you plagued by the memory of previous mistakes? You need to remember that you change and develop as a person as you gain more experience and that past mistakes do not mean that you will repeat them.

Lets face it, most of us will experience nerves in a situation which is stressful to us. This is totally normal and quite often we become anxious and charged with adrenaline which drives us on. When it comes to speaking in public the adrenaline can be positive but excessive nerves are negative and can lead to aggression.

Fundamentally, the key to successful public speaking is the acquisition of confidence coupled with assertiveness which leads to the ability to effectively control a situation. If you are assertive and you know your subject  matter you are likely to be confident and in control and less likely to feel nervous.

## Be prepared!

Directly related to the above, preparation is everything and to feel confident with your material means that you are half way there already. Although I will be expanding on preparation a little later, there are a few fundamental tips which can help you along.

You should listen to speakers, particularly good speakers as often as possible in order to gain tips. Notice the way that  good and effective speakers construct their sentences. Listen for the eloquence. Remember, shorter sentences have a lot more impact and are easier to grasp than long sentences. They also act a discipline for the speaker in that they will prevent him or her from straying off the point.

Another very important tip when approaching the day of your presentation is preparing yourself psychologically. Convince yourself that you are looking forward to the speech and that you will do well no matter what. Convey this to your audience as you open your presentation, say that you are glad to be with them and that you hope that this goes well for all. This reinforces a feeling of goodwill and will express itself through your body language and your voice.

Finally, one of the main aids to effective public speaking is *experience* and that only comes through practice so it is essential that you take every opportunity offered you to sharpen your skills in this area.

In the next chapter I will be concentrating on presentation and style. Fundamental to preparation as a speaker is the ability to relax and focus your mind and body on the task ahead.

# 2

# PRESENTING MATERIAL

## PERSONAL SKILLS

### Body Language

People have a natural ability to use body language together with speech. Body language emphasises speech and enables us to communicate more effectively with others. It is vitally important when preparing for the role of public speaker to understand the nature of your body language and also to connect this to another all important element-*vision*.

### Vision

People tend to take in a lot of information with their eyes and obviously presentations are greatly enhanced by use of visual aids. Together, when presenting to a group of people, as a public speaker, *body language and visual stimuli* are all important. A great amount of thought needs to go into the elements of what it is that you are about to present and the way you intend to convey your message. What you should not do, especially as a novice, is to stand up in front of a group and deliver a presentation off the top of your head. You need to carry out thorough research into what it is you are presenting and to whom you are presenting.

### Developing a style

Every person engaged in public speaking will have his or her own style. At the one end of the spectrum there are those people who give no thought to what it is they are doing and have no real interest in the audience. For them it is a chore and one which should be gotten over as soon as is possible. Such public speakers can be slow, boring and ineffectual leaving only traces of annoyance in the audiences mind. Here, there is a definite absence of style.

At the other end of the spectrum are those who have given a great deal of thought to what they are doing, given a great deal of thought to their material and have a genuine interest in the audience. Such public speakers will be greatly stimulating and leave a lasting impression and actually convey something of some worth.

*It does not matter what the occasion of your public speaking role is, wedding (best mans speech etc.) seminar, presentation to employers. The principles are the same-that is understanding your material, understand the nature of yourself as you relate to the material and how this will translate into spoken and body language and also how you will use visual aids to enhance the presentation.*

Underlying all of this is your *own personal style*, partly which develops from an understanding of the above and partly from an understanding of yourself. Some presenters of material recognise their own speed of presentation, i.e. slow, medium or fast and also understand their own body language. Some are more fluent than others, use their hands more etc. Having recognized your own style what you need to do is to adjust your own way of presentation to the specific requirements of the occasion. The key point is to gain attention, get the  message across and be stimulating to a degree. Obviously some occasions are more formal than others. You should study the nature of the occasion and give a lot of thought to what is required, i.e. degree of humor, seriousness etc. All of the above considerations begin to translate themselves into a style which you yourself will begin to recognize and feel comfortable with. Once this occurs you will find that, when presenting, your nerves will begin to melt away and your confidence begins to develop

## Formal presentations

As this is a book about public speaking, with the emphasis on the more formal setting, we should now concentrate on the various elements which go to make up a successful presentation to a group.

There is not one particular style appropriate to public speaking. Each occasion will merit its own approach. However, there are a few commonly observed rules.

## Use of language

The use of language is a specific medium which must be understood when making a presentation. Obviously, if you are speaking publicly to a group of familiar people who know and understand you, a different approach will be needed and a different form of language, perhaps less formal, utilized than that used in front of a group who are totally unfamiliar.

Nevertheless, using formal but simple language interspersed with funny remarks is undoubtedly one of the best ways to approach any form of audience, friends or not. You should certainly avoid too much detail and do not go overboard with funny comments as this will become tedious. Stick to the subject matter lightening up the occasion with a few anecdotes and witty comments. It is all about the right blend and pitch.

## Body Language

We have briefly discussed body language. It is astounding how much you can tell about people in the street by simply observing their body language. Usually people form an impression about another within the first five minutes of meeting. It is essential, in a public speaking situation that your body language should reflect a confident personality with a good sense of humor. In order to achieve this you should think about the following:

**Use of hands**

- Use your hands to emphasize what you say and to invite the audience to accept your point

- Keep your hands open and keep your fingers open.

- Avoid putting your hands in your pocket and avoid closing them. Firmly avoid pointing fingers

- co-ordinate your hand movements with your words.

## Using facial expressions

People tend to concentrate on the face of a public speaker, in addition to the movements of the body. Obviously, your face, along with body language is a vehicle for expression. A smile every now and again is important. There are other actions which can help:

- Use of eyebrows for inviting people to accept your ideas

- Moving the head to look at all members of a group. Very important indeed to maintain a sense of involvement on the part of all

- Do not fix your eyes on one place or person for long. This will isolate the rest of the audience and may be interpreted as nervousness or a lack of confidence on your part

- Look at individuals every time you mention something in their area of expertise or are singling them out in a positive way

- Look at people even if they appear not to be looking at you

*The face is a very important part of the communication apparatus and the use of this part of the body is of the utmost importance when public speaking.*

## Controlling your movements

In addition to the use of face and hands the way you move can have an effect on your audience. Your movements can vary from standing rigid and fixed to acting out roles and being fluid generally. There are, in. keeping with body language generally, certain rules relating to movement:

* Restrict your movements only to those which are most necessary. Avoid throwing yourself all over the place and distracting peoples attention from the emphasis of your presentation

* Always face the people that you are addressing. Never look at the floor or away from the audience, at least not for a prolonged period of time

## Dress

When adopting the role of public speaker it is very important to be dressed formally and in accordance with the standard of the occasion, or the nature of the occasion. Dressing formally does not mean automatically wearing a suit and tie. It does mean however that you should think in terms of power dressing. This means that you wish to make an impression on people, not just through what you say and do, not just through your body language or visual presentations but by the way you look. People must be impressed. This means that you must give thought to what you wear, how you can help to achieve a sense of control through dress.

## Attitude

Your attitude is crucial to your success in public speaking. Attitudes can be greatly influenced by nerves and by being ill prepared. There is nothing worse than a public speaker who slowly degenerates into aggression or hostility through sarcasm or other forms of attack. Yet this is all too frequent. At all times you must maintain a professional and formal attitude which allows you to remain in control. You can think yourself into this state if you find yourself slipping or feel that you are losing control.

If you feel that you are straying in any way then you should get back on course. This can be achieved through a number of ways such as by changing the subject slightly in order to give yourself time to gather your wits or by asking the group to refocus on the subject in question.

Attitude is also disciplined by self composure which can be engendered through relaxation which in turn is brought about by understanding the role of exercise and meditation, which we will be elaborating on a little later.

## Formalities

Another fundamental rule of presentations is the way you open or introduce the presentation and the way you close. When public speaking it is always necessary to introduce yourself even if most of the audience know who you are. It is vital that everyone knows who you are, who you represent, if anybody, and what you are there for. Having got these necessary formalities over with the audience will feel more comfortable listening to you because they now have a point of reference.

Depending on the situation, you may even want to ask the audience if they would like to introduce themselves, through a "round robin" which entails each person telling you and the others who they are and what they hope to get out of the presentation. This approach however, is only really necessary and useful in seminar or teaching situations. Such an approach would be wholly inappropriate in a speech situation.

## Practicing presentations

*Taking into account all of the above and then practicing.* This is the absolute key to successful presentations and to effective public speaking. Practice most certainly lifts your confidence level up and assists you in staying in control The more time and effort that you spend practicing the less that you will have to worry about when presenting. Lets face it, a presentation is a live stage show. How do stand up comics feel when they expose themselves to an audience? Develop a practicing technique by trying different methods:

- You should choose a topic that you are very interested in and prepare a short presentation on it.

- Stand in front of a mirror and present to yourself. Repeat this over and over observing different aspects of your style.

- Try to rectify any bad habits.

- Experiment with various styles and techniques until you find one that suits you.

- Try to film yourself if possible. Replay the film and observe yourself. This is one of the most effective ways of changing your style, or developing your style.

- Ask a friend to observe you and to make detailed criticism. Do not be afraid of criticism as this is always constructive

At this point you should be concentrating on style only. Do not worry about content as we will be discussing this a little later.

.

# 3

# PREPARINGFOR PRESENTATION.

## Carrying out effective research

Having considered some of the personal skills needed in order to become an effective public speaker, we now need to concentrate on the nature of the material used. Remember, the most important elements of public speaking are the person delivering the speech/presentation and the material.

When you are faced with the task of public speaking, which involves presentation of material, any material, then the first point to be aware of is that you will need to carry out some sort of research. Although you may feel fairly well versed in the area in question, it is always advisable to do a little research. This counts for speeches at a wedding as well as more complex presentations in front of a group of people.

There are certain fundamental questions which should be asked before researching any topic. The first one is, how much do you know about the topic and who are you presenting to? How long are you presenting for and when and where is the presentation taking place?

## Gathering information/identification of sources

Gathering information can be time consuming and requires effort. However, if you wish to ensure that you have quality information relevant to the topic in hand then this cannot be avoided. Start by identifying the topics that you are covering and work out various ways of getting appropriate materials. Once you know what you need then you need to carry out checks on the different locations, i.e., libraries, universities etc.

You need to ensure that you have effective ways of storing data. This is quite important and there are several key ways of ensuring that you stay organized:

- File the information that you have researched and index the file

- If you have ready access to a computer, save any information on the database and create easy to follow search fields

- Use key search words to classify the information, and divide each file into sub-files.

Any of the above are suitable for organizing your information, manual or computerized. The most important thing is to be able to retrieve it readily.

**Filtering and assembling the information**

Once you feel that you have enough information then you have to decide how much of it you want to use. Great care should be to ensure that your material is to the point, covers all angles but is not overladen with unnecessary facts.

Once you have decided what topics the presentation is going to include, it is important to put it into words that you can remember, or feel comfortable with when you are giving your talk. Getting started is

always difficult. The introduction to a speech or presentation is the most difficult part and it is the point where you may be overtaken by

nerves. It is worth leaving this part of your speech or presentation to the end so that you have worked through the main body and can then assemble a knowledgeable beginning.

Do not try to achieve perfection with your presentation or you may end up a bag of nerves and end up spending more time than you had anticipated without really achieving the desired end.

You should always prepare a script in the first instance. It could be that you wish to memorize the material and deliver an off the cuff presentation to your audience. However, it is always advisable to write a script. Having a script, or a crib sheet as a framework helps you avoid the dangers of trying to improvise which can lead you into a corner and undermine your confidence if you lose track of what you are saying. Ideally, your level of comfort with the content of your presentation should be the sum of your level of knowledge of the subject and the level of your preparation.

## The script writing process

The following is one way of preparing a script which is effective but simple.

*Preparing a first draft*

- Start developing your ideas into a short story

- Rely on your memory to start with to see what you can put together without referring to your notes. This helps you clarify your ideas and find out how much you know about the subject.

- Refer to your notes when you get stuck.

- Try to find any points that you failed to recollect.

- Do not, at this stage, worry about your style and grammar as this will confuse you and delay your thinking process.

*Pulling the second draft together*

The second draft requires a more detailed approach. It is now time to look at the structure of the script and see whether the transition between sections takes place smoothly. If two consecutive ideas are not related, the shift between them becomes noticeable and the presentation loses its continuity. Try to find a link or a point in common with the two ideas and insert it between them.

Apply the following steps when you work on your second draft:

- Put the different sections in the right order to facilitate smooth transition between them.

- Add the right sentences at the beginning and end of each section for a smooth transition

- Read the script out loud to get a feel of what it sounds like.

After checking the transitions, it is time to divert your attention towards the grammar.

- Make the tone sound formal but do not take it to extremes. This will very much depend on what you are presenting. However, if you are presenting to a large group and the presentation is report style then you should always be formal.

- Avoid expressing yourself in a negative way and use positive terms whenever you can.

- Using factual language reflects a friendly and convincing tone. Extravagant expressions can only serve to confuse the listener.

## Dealing with excessive information

An important factor which may affect the length of your script is the time that you have available to you. It is very important to keep to the time allowed. One of the major contributors to nerves is overrunning the length of time that you have.

One of the most common problems with report style presentations is to include a large amount of information, within a short time, which can be very confusing to the audience. If your script is obviously too long, edit it by removing details and leaving highlights of the important points.

Conversely, you may find that you do not have enough material to present. One of the most common solutions here, again within a report style presentation is to ask questions of the audience to fill in time.

## The final draft

When all these changes are complete, you will have a final draft of your presentation. It is now up to you to learn to deliver it as a talk. Whatever you try to do, try to be as natural as you possibly can. If you are making a formal presentation then try to use graphic illustrations to

ensure that the message is getting home. Obviously, if you are making a speech at a wedding then this is inappropriate.

# 4

# THE USE OF VISUAL AIDS

Before we further discuss presentation of your material it is necessary to talk a little about the use of visual aids.

Visual aids are used for effect, for helping you to make your point. They offer audiences a visual representation of what you are trying to put across. Generally, you can explain a point much quicker with the use of visual aids.

Visual aids also keep audiences interested as there is more entertainment value with the use of visual images than there is with the spoken word. Combined with words, visual aids help you to communicate ideas in a very short time and leave a longer lasting impression on the audience. This is only true, though, if you use them to their best effect. The opposite can have a detrimental effect on the audience.

Visual aids are not effective if they are not prepared very carefully together with the script that you are presenting. Do not try to overload the visual aid in terms of its contents or this will, more often than not, confuse your audience. Whether you use a graph, diagram or picture on the slide (if it is a slide that you are using) then put only one on each slide. When working on the main body of the slide keep the following in mind:

- Keep it as simple as possible

- Use pictures as often as you can keeping text to a minimum

- Leave plenty of space between items for visibility

- Use professional images (computer generated) as opposed to hand drawn.

Throughout your presentation, try to use the same style for visual aids.

## Presenting with visual images

Images are there to help you and you should be comfortable with using the equipment which displays them. The following tips are useful when presenting:

- Ignore the existence of a picture behind you. Never turn your back on the audience. Talk to them at the same time as they are looking at the image

- Always rehearse with your visual aids. This will help you to familiarize yourself with the equipment and also to remember the sequence in which you will present the slides

- If you are going to use an overhead projector, make sure that all your acetates are in order. Put them back in the same order when you finish so that they are ready for use the next time. Keep them clean.

- Stand to one side of the overhead projector when you are presenting. Use a pointer to make a relevant point. Let the audience see where you are pointing your pointer.

## Tools for the presentation of visual aids

## Use of an Overhead projector

This particular tool is the most popular of all visual aids. It is widely used in all forms of presentations because of its flexibility. It can be used to project almost any form of material.

# Slide projectors

This is the second most popular tool for visual aids The quality is always very good, often much better than the OHP. However, it can be more expensive to produce materials than the OHP.

# Using a video

This is the most effective visual aid but should be used only for limited periods. More information can be shown in a short space of time than other forms of visual aid.

# Use of a monitor view pad

This is a relatively new method of projection. The device has a transparent liquid display screen which, when connected to a computer acts as a monitor. The screen can then be placed on an OHP to replace an acetate. This is slightly more technical and long winded than the OHP on its own but the results can be very professional.

# Use of other visual aids

In addition to the main method chosen by yourself there are other peripheral visual aids which you may wish to utilize. The following are also quite effective:

- *Flip chart.* This particular tool enables you to write and draw as you go along. Also very useful if you wish people to break into groups in order to carry out an exercise.

- *models and prototypes.* Showing a model is very powerful when trying to demonstrate a particular point. Displaying models of buildings can be more effective than showing plans.

**Use of color**

Color is also a very powerful medium when you wish to make important information stand out. The audience can focus on the colored parts with the background information remaining in the background.

**Working with computers**

Computers are playing an increasingly important part in presentations. Whether you are making or presenting slides, the results look more professional and effective with the use of presentation or graphics software.

**Choosing the right equipment**

It is important to use the right kind of visual aids for each occasion. If used incorrectly, visual aids can give the wrong impression or even ruin your chances of success in getting your message across. Choosing the right visual aid is quite difficult. The following are points to consider:

- The ability to grab the audiences attention. There is no point in using the most impressive equipment if it will not appeal to the audience

- The suitability for the occasion. You do not need to use state of the art equipment if you are giving a short speech. Use the most appropriate form of equipment

- The effect of your visual aids on the audience. Will the visual aid that you intend to use help or just confuse the audience. You should very carefully ensure that what you use perfectly compliments your presentation.

## Use of notes and handouts

It is sometimes useful to provide your audience with a handout of your presentation, or part of your presentation. This very much depends on what you are presenting. Only provide handouts when needed and not at the start of the presentation as this will distract the audience from what it is you are trying to say and also the content of any visual aid.

## Involving the audience

Sometimes you may wish to involve the audience in an interactive presentation. If you need to make a quick survey or opinion poll to prove a point, you can pass a short questionnaire to the audience and let someone help you in counting the votes and presenting.

Always remember, visual aids are there to assist you in presenting your message and if they don't achieve that don't bother with them.

# 5
## USING YOUR VOICE

We need to consider one of the most important aspects of public speaking before we move on to actual presentation.

What you say is very important indeed. However, even more important is the way that you say it. The right combination of body language and voice is far more potent than a clever and witty script. The two combined can help you become a very effective public speaker indeed.

### The voice

The voice plays a very important role in presentation and public speaking generally. The way you pitch your voice is guaranteed to either keep peoples attention or send them to sleep.

The voice is a result of air coming out of your lungs which causes the vocal chords to vibrate, producing different sounds. These various sounds are shaped into words by the speech organism in the head.

The brain then sends messages controlling the breathing and the tension of the vocal chords. Cavities in the body, such as the mouth and chest, provide amplification. The amplified sounds are then shaped into recognizable speech by the tongue, lips teeth etc. Speech is produced in two different ways:

- Voiced sounds-produced by speech organs in the mouth closer to the vocal chords at the back end of the tongue

- Unvoiced sounds-produced mainly using the tongue and front teeth. The sound of the letter S is produced in this way.

All the above aspects of voice and speech are controlled by the body organs that are unique to each person. We can develop the ability to control these organs to produce the speech that we want. This can be achieved by training the various muscles that produce and shape sounds. The shape of various cavities, such as the chest, can be changed to vary the level of sound amplification.

## Developing your voice

It is perfectly possible, and probably essential to improve on four characteristics of your speech:

- tone

- pitch

- volume

- clarity.

## Tone

If you restrict your body cavities responsible for amplifying sound, your voice will sound restricted and sometimes nasal. Restriction of body cavities can happen by standing or sitting in the wrong way.
*It is essential that you give thought to your posture and bearing when public speaking.*

## Pitch

As you stretch and loosen your voice chords, the pitch of your voice will change. When stretched, the number of vibrations increases due to the small distance allowed for them to vibrate. These vibrations produce high frequency (pitch) sounds. When the vocal chords are loose, more distance is allowed for them to vibrate which makes them produce low frequency (pitch) sounds.

# Volume

The volume of your voice can be improved in two ways. The first is by simply increasing the pressure of air coming out of your lungs, or by narrowing the space between the vocal chords (glottis). You can change the volume of a whisper simply by increasing the amount of air through your glottis which is widely open. Try to shout. You will notice that your glottis contracts sharply, to increase the volume of your voice.

# Clarity

To get your message across you need to say it clearly. Clarity is determined by the speech organs and how well you can control them. If you are too nervous your tongue and lips start playing tricks on you because they are tense. In order to speak clearly, overcome the problems associated with speech organs and get your message across.

Don't be scared of moving your lips. Exercise your speech muscles. Make sure that you pronounce things clearly and that you carry your voice.

# Voice pitch

People generally feel more comfortable listening to a deep voice, one that is well rounded and smooth. However, it is important to ensure that your voice is at your natural pitch and not forced. To find Your natural pitch, concentrate on the following exercises:

- Speak at the lowest note that feels comfortable to you

- Use a musical instrument, e,.g. a guitar or piano and find the note that corresponds to your lowest comfortable pitch

- Move four notes up the musical scale. This should be very close to your natural pitch

- Try to tune your voice with this note and speak with the music helping you to stay in tune

- Practice this as many times as you need, in order to become confident in finding your natural pitch quite quickly.

When you have found the natural pitch of your voice, you will need to work on some variations to make your speech more natural. Changing the pitch up and down according to the contents of the speech helps you to keep the audience attracted to what you are saying. Try saying a few sentences out loud and practice varying the pitch. You can then notice the relation between the contents of the sentences and your pitch when saying each of them. When you realize what you are capable of achieving with your voice, you can then consciously start varying the pitch.

Singing is very good for voice training and realizing the potential of your voice organs. Reading out loud and trying to act a story is also good training.

**Use of silences and pauses**

Sometimes, silence can be more effective than words. It is useful to pause every now and again to allow the listeners to absorb the ideas that you have put across. A short pause gives the audience time to absorb what you have said. You can also use pauses to help you relax and breath. Pauses also help you put your ideas together to start elaborating on a new point.

**A few useful hints on the use of pauses:**

- Don't feel compelled to fill the silence. If you find yourself speaking quickly for no real reason, force yourself to pause. Sometimes you may be very enthusiastic about what you are saying and find yourself speaking rapidly. Pause and use your body language and voice to show your enthusiasm

- Avoid becoming a slow speaker. Moderate the speed of your talk to the level of its contents. Always remember that the aim is to be understood and not to say as many words as possible within the given time

- Try to maintain the rhythm and the rate of flow of ideas throughout your presentation. Again this can be achieved by practicing your presentation enough times to make you feel confident and in command.

## Emphasis

There are other ways to emphasize a point or an idea. The amount of stress put on a syllable can also emphasize the word. You should say certain sentences, placing emphasis on different words. A few examples are:

- Can I have that *chair* please

- Can I have *that* chair please

In the first sentence you are asking for the chair and not something else. In the second sentence, you want the chair to be given to you and not someone else. Therefore, placing the stress on a word can change the whole sentence.

Avoid putting emphasis on too many words. This diminishes the effect of the technique and renders it useless.

It is important to realize that emphasis in many cases is placed on a group of words rather than just one. The same technique applies, but in the case of a group of words, the pitch change to the decisive tone can be extended to include all the words in the group. The whole group should be treated as one entity with the emphasis on the group and not the individual words.

## Voice projection

Voice projection depends on two main factors:

- Physical

- Psychological

The physical factor comprises

- The force with which you breathe

- The muscular power you put into forming the words

- The clarity of your pronunciation

If you get all these factors right then you will have no problem in projecting your voice. However, some people feel nervous in front of an audience and they fail to project their voice properly. In a lot of cases, speakers project their voices too much or too little simply because they do not look at the audience and estimate the power that they need to project. In order to estimate projection, you should look at the person the furthest away from you and imagine that you are talking too him or her. You will feel the need to project your voice to that person and be able to control your vocal organs and breathing accordingly.

## Use of the body

To help you to project your voice, you should make use of the resonance of your body cavities. Try the following:

- Relax the muscles in your neck and stand comfortably without bending or over straightening your chest.

- Also relax the muscles in your neck by nodding gently a few times.

- Take a deep breath and exhale, letting out a deep sound. You can then realize how the cavity in your chest resonates giving out a sigh of relief.

## The nose

A clear nose helps you to speak clearly and project your voice. If your nose is blocked, it is harder for you to pronounce certain letters let alone project your voice. It is also easier to breathe through a clear nose and therefore maintain the breathing rhythm.

## Improving posture

Other cavities in the body, such as the chest, can be used to create more resonance. It helps if your posture is right. For a good posture try the following:

Relax your muscles especially around the shoulder area. To do so you need to raise your shoulders and drop them a few times.

- Do not bend forward as you speak. This prevents your chest cavity from resonating

- If you stand with a curved back and too stiff you will not be able to project your voice properly

- Relax your body and stand in a natural position. This will help you not only project your voice but maintain it for a longer time too.

**Training and looking after your voice**

To change your speech habits which you have developed over a number of years, is not a simple matter. You need to consciously work at this before the changes become second nature to you. You should always look after your voice in order to maintain it:

- Avoid smoky rooms

- Allow your voice to rest. Even when you are giving a long talk or speech, you can still rest your voice by regular breathing and proper articulation

- Avoid warm and dry rooms which can bring on a sore throat

- Don't eat dairy products before your presentation, because the production of mucus is increased which roughens the voice

- If you feel that you have a dry mouth and throat, bite your tongue gently. This will produce enough saliva to wet your mouth.

- After a long talk, practice a few relaxing exercises to prepare your voice for rest. These exercises can be stretching, breathing articulation etc.

# 6

# THE IMPORTANCE OF EXERCISE

## Exercises to help you relax

Although at first glance exercising may seem to have very little to do with public speaking, in fact the reverse is true. There are certain exercises which are essential to your posture and general well-being. If you are aware of these simple routines and can go through the motions just prior to embarking on public speaking, then you will feel so much better.

## Shoulders

In order to feel relaxed, you should stand in a relaxed position, lift the shoulders and tense them. Slowly relax them by letting them fall. You should then note the difference in the way you feel. Sometimes we lift our shoulders and tense them without realizing that we are doing so. When your shoulders are tense, the neck becomes tense and you can feel very uncomfortable and tire more easily.

## Neck

Neck exercises are very beneficial in the process of relaxation. Move your head gently round from left to right in a circular motion. Imagine that you are repeating this exercise in front of an audience. This is particularly useful for releasing tension and should be carried out just prior to beginning your presentation.

## Head

In a standing position, let the head very slowly fall onto your chest. Repeat this for a few times and you feel very light and relaxed. The contrast between lightness and the heaviness which is experienced when your head is kept in a normal position over prolonged periods of time can be felt very easily.

## Concentration

This particular exercise is useful for focusing the mind. Choose an interesting object that appeals to you. Fix your mind on it taking in as much detail as possible. Rest your head against the back of the chair, close your eyes and place the image of that object in your mind. When you are ready, open your eyes. Carrying out this particular exercise is useful prior to public speaking.

## Breathing control

Breathing for any form of presentation is a natural function that we do not normally think about. If you find it difficult to project your voice in public, concentrating on the breathing aspects will work wonders for you.

To be heard by an audience, we need to create space in the throat and chest so that the required amount of air can be freely inhaled. When

using the voice, the exhaled air is directed through the vocal cords. The throat mouth and nose help us to amplify our sound. The mouth and throat should therefore be free of tension, and the nose kept clear and unlocked for the resonators to operate effectively.

## Breathing in

For this exercise, you should stand straight but not stiffly. Good posture helps promote strong voice production. Remember when you inhale not to raise the shoulders. Doing so will encourage tension in the neck, throat and breathing muscles.

Now you should feel your ribcage. Ribs form the thorax and are attached at the back to the twelve thoracic vertebrae. Rest one hand on your midriff and the other on your lower ribs that reach around the waist. Breathe in slowly and notice how the hand resting on the midriff moves out slightly. This has happened because the diaphragm, which is a muscular partition that separates the thorax from the abdomen, has contracted and flattened, thereby pushing the belly outwards. Because the lower ribs are more flexible than those higher up, they will flex outwards and upwards by the use of intercostal muscles that are attached to them.

This muscular activity expands the chest cavity, creating more space for the lungs to fill up with air, which is drawn into them through the windpipe, nose and/or mouth.

**Breathing out**

You should now breath out very slowly and feel the lower ribs gradually relax as the lungs contract. The diaphragm rises and the midriff or belly moves inwards. As this is happening, the abdominal muscles are gently drawn inwards. This contraction of the abdominal muscles is used to help our outgoing breath when we speak, gently

supporting the diaphragm and lower ribs, so that sound can be sustained and energized.

Because it is on the outgoing breath that we speak, we aim to balance breath with sound. The moment we start to exhale, we need to use the voice. This can be achieved by humming. This will help you to attain a smoothness.

Physical tensions and feelings of nervousness can be increased or even caused by insufficient intake of air. At times, this can result in a sore throat, breathy or strained voice and tailing off at the ends of sentences. Some speakers do not allow themselves breathing space. They take in small gasps of air and do not take advantage of their breathing muscles. The shoulders may rise on inhalation, which encourages the ribs to move one way only-vertically- and this can constrict the breath. The ribs need to flex vertically and laterally. Raising the arms slightly to the side while practicing breathing in may provide a picture of opening out, so that lateral expansion is encouraged.

**The voice generally**

As we have discussed, when speaking in public, the voice needs to be strong and powerful without straining or shouting. You need to get the message home to people in a clear confident way. Your breath is the power behind your voice. It is important to inhale as much as possible The aim is to flow and we breath when there are pauses in the text.

In order to make sense of content, learn where to punctuate your speech and phrase your words. Do not break your phrases or your speech will become jerky and the sense may be lost.

When your speech is prepared, practice it aloud and initially gauge where you are going to take:

• Your full stop pauses

• Your comma pauses and supplementary breaths

Ensure that you are standing straight but be at ease, especially around the top part of your body, the neck, throat and shoulders, which should be relaxed and down. Stand with legs slightly apart, the weight evenly distributed on both feet. Your head needs to be well balanced between the shoulder blades. The chin should not jut out or be pushed too far into the neck. If you were speaking to a fairly large audience you would need to speak a little slower and very clearly.

The above represent a few key exercises which you should become familiar with if you wish to increase your effectiveness as a public speaker and become aware of your posture and your physical self generally.

# 7
# THE IMPORTANCE OF SETTING

By now, you should have gained a reasonably clear idea of the ground work that you must do before you are ready to stand in front of others and make an effective presentation. In addition, you will have gained some idea of the importance of physical exercise and its relation to your own well being. However, before you do begin your presentation it will do no harm in considering the type of environment that you will present in.

**Choosing the right setting**

There are a number of types of place where you may find yourself giving a presentation. These can vary from a small over ventilated room to a large and comfortable seminar room. For a good setting a room should possess the following:

- It should be large enough to accommodate all present

- The temperature should be just right and not uncomfortable (too hot or too warm)

- All seats should be positioned correctly

- Enough space should be provided for visual aids

- Lighting should be controllable

- There should be enough power points close to the location of your equipment

- The acoustics should be suitable.

If you have the chance to go into a room some time before the presentation, look out for aspects which can be improved upon and which bring the room in line with the above criteria.

## *Further tips are:*

- close any windows which overlook a busy street, to avoid noise pollution in the room. If the room is too warm and you need to open a window, do so before the presentation and close them just before you start

- If the room is small, with an elevated platform for the presenter to stand on, arrange the seating to give you enough space in front of the platform. Use this space and avoid standing at a higher level than your small audience. This can only intimidate them and create barriers

- If you can rearrange the seating in the room, always try to place the seats facing you with their back to the room door. This enables latecomers to sneak in  without distracting peoples attention from you

- In large lecture theaters, make sure that the lighting is controlled, so that when you start your presentation, it is dimmed in the audience section. This helps the audience focus on you and your visual aids.

- However, it should not be too dark for the audience to take notes if necessary.

# AND FINALLY!

# DELIVERING YOUR PRESENTATION!

# 8

# DELIVERING YOUR PRESENTATION

You are at the point where your speech has been written and your visual and other aids have been prepared. You have also acquired knowledge about your personal self and also your setting. If possible, you should allow yourself time for a dress rehearsal prior to delivering your speech. Of course, a dress rehearsal may not be necessary on all occasions. However, if you are speaking in front of a lot of people then you may want to at least spend some time taking in the area you will speak in and also to run through a few motions.

## Lighting

Check on the lighting. Make sure that there is ample lighting and that it does not shine in your eyes.

## Microphones

For rooms and smaller venues the natural voice can be used. However, for larger halls a microphone is essential. When you are using a microphone keep your head about four inches away when you speak. Avoid any feedback or handling noise.

## Appearance

As we mentioned earlier aim at being comfortable and smart. For the woman:

Keep the hair away from the face, so that it is not masked, but retain a soft style

Earrings can soften the face and add interest, but avoid the large dangling variety; they will be a distraction

A colorful scarf or brooch adds a touch of sophistication and interest to the neckline

Avoid wearing dull colors unless they are offset by something bright and cheerful

Check that your hemlines are straight especially if wearing a full skirt.

## For the man

Wear a well fitting suit and shirt with the cuffs just showing below the jacket. The tie should be neatly tied.

Black shoes are preferable to brown; brown tends to distract the eye. Colored dark socks should be worn, rather than white. Make sure that the socks cover the calves adequately.

You should smile as often as possible because this gives the impression of being confident.

## Final tips

Listen while you are waiting your turn. Focus on the other speakers if you can.

## Walking onto the platform (or standing up)

Make a good first impression. This will work wonders for your confidence. If you are walking up to a platform, adopt an easy gait with your arms swinging naturally and your body straight.

Show your audience that you are happy to be there, by being warm and relaxed. Animate your body movements. Positive body language is very important. If you are using a lectern, place your notes on it with a quick glance down, and then look at your audience. Smile as you make your opening remarks. This way you appear much more approachable and attractive.

Focus on your audience. When there is a large audience present, it is sometimes difficult to know where to look when making a speech. If there is strong stage lighting, it is unlikely that you will be able to see your audience, in which case individual eye contact is impossible. If there is a central exit light at the back of the hall, use that as your main focus point. In between times, the eye can travel to the right hand side of the hall and then the left, always homing back to the exit sign. This gives the illusion of looking at the audience.

**Achieving smooth and effective presentations**

When you address an audience, in a formal setting, you should always state your name and what it is that you are about to present. This should always head your script. However, if you are going to be introduced by someone else or you are very well known to the audience, you can start in a different way. There are certain

fundamental tips that you should take into account when planning. Consider first the mood that your audience is likely to be in. Take the appropriate action for each of the following attitudes of the audience:

- Waiting for you to start. There is no need to capture your audiences attention start when you are ready.

- Expected to disagree with your statements. Do not make matters worse by starting with an announcement that can only worsen the situation.

- Indifferent audience. For this type of audience, you need to be controversial. Start with something which provokes their interest and forces them to listen to you.

After assessing the audience, depending on who is going to be present, you have to decide on the type of opening to use. There are several types of introduction for the situations described above, and here are some effective openings:

- Start straight by involving the audience through questions that will make them think about the subject that you are presenting. For example, "Good Morning, were you in a traffic jam this morning and had no way of communicating the fact that you were going to be late?. This could be the opener for a talk about some form of communication, for example, the mobile phone.

- Start with an unexpected or controversial statement to seize the attention of the audience.

- Thank the person who introduced you, if he or she is known to the audience. Also, thank the organizers of the event or the people who invited you to give a presentation.

Use these examples as a brief guide and choose the right words for the right situation. It is important to memorize the opening lines because this is the most difficult bit of a presentation. If you get them right then all will usually be plain sailing. If you get them wrong then it may take you time to recover your composure.

**Explaining the main points of your presentation**

After you have managed to gain their attention you should begin to plan the conveyance of the main part of your text, or script or message. After the introduction, you should tell the audience what you are going to be telling them in the next few minutes. The following steps should be taken:

- Start by saying a few words about the content of the presentation. Mention the most important points and don't cram the slides with headings of the various sections of the script. Avoid using too many words, especially on the first slide.

- Later in your presentation, give them a reminder of what has been said.

- Bear in mind that people can only concentrate for ten to fifteen minutes. Keep them interested by timing your funny remarks to coincide with the audiences weak moments. Don't spoil your joke by letting them know that you are going to tell one. Make sure that your jokes are highly relevant, and don't bring in any old story just for the sake of being funny, as people will wonder about its relevance.

- Another way of getting peoples attention back is to ask them direct questions. If you notice that someone is on the verge of sleeping, you can look at them as you ask the question.

## Choosing your closing words

Your last words in the presentation have to be remembered by the audience. Your conclusion is your chance to achieve this. It certainly is not the place to introduce new ideas. Your conclusion may cover things related to the introduction and the content of the presentation such as what course of action was taken or what can be done in the future. Think hard about what thoughts you want the audience to leave the room with.

## Questions from the audience

This is your chance to get positive feedback from the audience. If the occasion is being chaired, and the chairperson is efficient, he or she will monitor the action. Alternatively, engage someone in the audience to set the ball rolling.

If a question is being asked too quietly, repeat it for the benefit of the audience. Also, you should rephrase a question that has been poorly expressed. If there is an awkward customer in the audience, try to keep cool. You should think very carefully about how you are going to handle the situation. If it is appropriate you should try asking a few questions.

## Accepting compliments

Sometimes, a public speaker gives such a good impression that the audience will applaud or give compliments. It is very important for the speaker to graciously accept these and not to reject them or appear negative. The end of the affair can be so much nicer if all feel appreciated.

Remember, be relaxed, be prepared, be spontaneous. Warm to the audience and get them to warm to you and be confident when you are

presenting. This will make the whole experience worthwhile and rewarding for all.

Use all of the tips that you have picked up throughout the book. Use visual aids to the best effect. Project your voice and involve people.

# 9
# REFLECTING ON YOUR PRESENTATION

It is now time to reflect, very briefly, on what has been emphasised throughout this book.

As was stated right at the outset, public speaking is very much an art and a skill which can be mastered by anyone. Some people may be initially better equipped than others for the role of public speaker, but anyone can become an effective speaker and master the art of presentation.

There are two vital ingredients in public speaking and, throughout this book, both aspects have been concentrated upon. *The person* needs to be aware and confident and the *material* needs to be well researched and appropriate to the occasion.

The person needs to be free of nerves and suitably relaxed, aware of his or her body language and also of style, which includes mode of dress.

The material which you are presenting needs to be well researched and organised and appropriate visual aids need to be available to enhance your material. If necessary, use notes and handouts to reinforce what you are saying.

You need to be aware of your voice and of how you deliver the material. Voice development in relation to public speaking is of the utmost importance. The tone, pitch, volume and clarity of your voice all need to be developed, along with the clarity.

Be aware of the setting in which the presentation is to be made, the size and layout plus the general acoustics. Lighting and amplification is also important.

Ensure that you are dressed well, make a good first impression when entering the room and handle the audience confidently and professionally.

The end product of all of the above advice is the delivery of a successful and effective presentation to your audience, whatever that presentation may be. This can be enormously gratifying. However, as we have seen, in order to master the art of public speaking, there is a lot of preparation.

Good luck.

# INDEX

## A

ADRENALINE  13

APPEARANCE  61

ASSEMBLING INFORMATION  25

ATTITUDE  22

## B

BODY LANGUAGE  19

BODY (USE OF)  21

BREATHING  50

BREATHING (CONTROL)  50

## C

CONFIDENCE  13

CONCENTRATION  50

CONTROL (OF MOVEMENTS)  21

COMPUTERS  36

CLARITY  41

# OTHER GUIDES IN THIS SERIES

**Other guides in the series:**

A Guide to:

Letting property
Small Claims in the County Court
Buying and selling Your own Home
Do It Yourself Divorce The Easyway
Bankruptcy and Company Insolvency
Accounts and Book-keeping for Small business
Business Planning
Writing a C.V and Conducting an Interview
Family Law
Setting up a Business
Negotiations the Easyway
The Rights of the Consumer
Guide to Employment Law
Bailiffs Powers-A Debtors Guide

# NOTES

# NOTES

# NOTES

**NOTES**

# NOTES

## NOTES

# NOTES

## NOTES

# NOTES

## NOTES

If you require any further information about Easyway guides or would like to contribute as an author please contact:

Easyway Guides
38 Cromwell Road
Walthamstow
London E17 9JN.